Candy
Bouquets

Create Your Own Gifts & Centerpieces

D0150672

Delicious Designs

Printed in the United States of America
by G&R Publishing Co.

Published By:

507 Industrial Street
Waverly, IA 50677

ISBN-13: 978-1-56383-299-4
ISBN-10: 1-56383-299-2
Item #3622

Table of Contents

Getting Started

It's a sweet feeling to treat your friends and family members to something special. That's why candy bouquets make such a great gift or party centerpiece.

The bouquet ideas provided in this book are easy, economical and fun to create. Look for variations, extra tips and colorful photos provided to make creating your masterpiece a little easier.

Who doesn't have a bit of sweet tooth? And, giving a gift that is beautiful as well as edible is a sure way to please anyone.

Food Safety

Before you begin your candy-coated creations, thoroughly wash your hands, the container or base as well as any utensils you may be using with soap and warm water. Even though some of these items may not be touching candy directly, you wouldn't want any dirt, germs or other unhealthy elements contaminating the bouquet.

Ingesting Styrofoam can be dangerous to one's health. When using Styrofoam as a base for an arrangement, always use wrapped candy.

Styrofoam dust or particles can attach to candy when arranging your bouquet so it's best to make sure candy is covered before you begin. If this is not an option, wrap the Styrofoam in plastic wrap or aluminum foil before inserting or attaching candy to it.

Supplies

Other than your favorite sweets and a cute container, some of the most common supplies used to make candy bouquets include Styrofoam, straight pins and a hot glue gun.

It is recommended that quilters T-pins be used because they are stronger and more durable than regular straight pins, although either will work. Some directions specifically list T-pins because an element of assembly would not work without them.

In addition some bouquet instructions indicate the exact size of Styrofoam piece needed for assembly because the base or container size is specific. Others are not specific because containers chosen may vary in size and width, making it easier to trim or cut a larger piece of Styrofoam to fit.

All supplies for these bouquets can be purchased at local supermarkets and discount stores.

Get Creative

Don't be afraid to think outside of the candy wrapper! Get creative with candy colors, wrappers, boxes and flavors.

When choosing containers, think seasonally or by the theme of your bouquet, and choose colors that complement each other. Find ribbon that brings out less prominent colors and/or enhances themes. The smallest details are those that can make or break your candy bouquet.

New Year's Kiss

New Year's Kiss

You will need:

- 1 (4″) Styrofoam ball
- 1 (4 ½″ tall) galvanized pail
- White shredded paper
- 1 (12″) wooden dowel
- 1 (6″) Styrofoam ball
- 1 (5″) Styrofoam ball

- Hot glue gun
- 2 (1 lb.) bags milk chocolate kisses
- 15 to 20 dark chocolate kisses
- 1 (36″) piece purple ribbon

To Begin...

1 Place the 4″ Styrofoam ball snugly in the galvanized pail. Cover ball with white shredded paper. Place the 5″ Styrofoam ball on the wooden dowel and slide it down to the center of the dowel. Then place the 6″ ball on the dowel above the 5″ ball so the balls rest 1½″ apart from each other. It is important to pierce Styrofoam balls with the dowel before you begin to attach candy kisses so when you're finished, the candy covered balls slide easily onto the dowel.

2 Apply hot glue on the end of the dowel and insert the dowel through the shredded paper into the center of the Styrofoam ball in the pail. The glue will dry and keep the dowel stable and in place. Remove both the 5″ and 6″ balls from the dowel. Set the pail aside. Making note of where the dowel holes are, cover both the 5″ and 6″ Styrofoam balls in aluminum foil. Once covered, poke a hole in the foil to expose the openings made for the dowel.

3 Apply a dot of hot glue to one chocolate kiss at a time. Then attach each kiss to the foil covered ball. Cover the 5″ ball completely with milk chocolate kisses. Alternate milk chocolate and dark chocolate kisses on the 6″ ball.

4 Apply a small dot of hot glue to both dowel openings on the 5″ ball. Slide the ball on the dowel to the center. Hold it for a few seconds to make sure the glue dries and the ball is secure. Apply a small dot of hot glue to the dowel opening of the 6″ ball. Slide the ball onto the dowel above the 5″ ball. Hold it for a few seconds to make sure the glue dries and the ball is secure.

5 Tie the purple ribbon into a bow. Using a straight pin, stick the bow to the top of the 5″ ball. It should appear that the bow is tied between the two balls.

Variations:

This festive topiary can be made with one, two or three balls of different sizes. It may also be placed in a larger pail or container. Try using various chocolate kiss flavors wrapped in different colors to create other holiday centerpieces.

You will need:

- Hot glue gun
- 1 (3″ x 2″) Styrofoam disk
- 1 (3⅞″ x 1¹⁵⁄₁₆″) Styrofoam disk
- 7 to 8 pieces grape Laffy Taffy
- 7 to 8 pieces apple Laffy Taffy
- 1 (11.5 oz.) package Tootsie Fruit Rolls
- 50 to 70 quilters T-pins or straight pins
- 1 Tootsie Pop sucker, any flavor

1 Using the hot glue gun, squeeze hot glue onto the bottom of the 3″ x 2″ Styrofoam disk. Glue the disk to the flat center of the larger disk. Squeeze hot glue on the back of one grape Laffy Taffy and attach the taffy to outside edge of the bottom Styrofoam disk. Line the end of the taffy up with the bottom of the disk so it sits level. The taffy wrappers on top will extend higher than the Styrofoam. Repeat with remaining taffy, alternating flavors and slightly overlapping the edges.

2 Insert a pin through one end of a Tootsie Roll wrapper. Push pin into Styrofoam to affix candy. Starting at the bottom just above the taffy, place the Tootsie Rolls in single rows around the outside and top of the smaller Styrofoam disk. Repeat until top and sides of disk are completely covered leaving only a small circle exposed at the top. Alternate Tootsie Roll flavors as desired.

3 Insert the Tootsie Pop into the center of the exposed area on the top Styrofoam piece. Gently press down until only the wrapper is exposed above the other candy.

You will need:

- 1 (1 lb.) bag Life Savers
- 1 (6″ tall) Styrofoam cone
- 75 to 125 quilters T-pins
- 2 to 3 (10″ to 12″) pieces ribbon and/or rick rack, various colors and patterns
- 8 to 10 small jingle bells

To Begin...

1 Insert a T-pin through one end of a Life Saver wrapper. Push the pin into the Styrofoam to affix candy to the cone. Place candies in a single row, circling the cone completely. Repeat until the cone is completely covered. Leave a small space at the very top of the cone exposed in order to decorate with ribbon.

2 Fold some of the ribbon pieces in half to create loops and leave others straight. Arrange your ribbon to look like a bow or other creative display. Place a pin in the center of the ribbon arrangement and affix to the top of the cone. Once attached, trim ribbon to fit cone as needed.

3 Insert T-pins through the bottom of the jingle bells and pull the sharp end through the opening on the other side. Affix one bell to the top of the cone, covering the center of the ribbon arrangement. Randomly place remaining jingle bells around the cone for an extra decorative accent.

Note: T-pins are best to use when decorating a centerpiece with Life Savers, especially when candy will be hanging from a Styrofoam cone. Because of the weight of the candy and flimsiness of the wrapper, regular straight pins have a tendency to rip or slide right through the plastic.

Gumball Machine

Gumball
Machine

You will need:

- Red spray paint
- 1 (7″) terra cotta pot
- 1 Styrofoam piece
- 1 (12″ to 14″ long) dowel
- Hot glue gun
- 1 (10″) Styrofoam ball

- 2½ (1 lb.) bags Dubble Bubble gum, assorted colors and flavors
- 10 to 12 hard red gumballs, AbracaBubble recommended

To Begin...

1 Spray the entire outside of the terra cotta pot with red paint. The pot will need at least three coats of paint; let dry for 1 to 2 hours. Trim the Styrofoam piece to fit snugly inside the pot.

2 Turn the pot upside down and insert the dowel into the small hole in the center of the pot's bottom. Press it all the way through so it pierces the Styrofoam. The Styrofoam will act as an anchor holding the dowel in place. Squeeze hot glue onto the bottom of the pot around the hole. Slide the Styrofoam ball onto the dowel and all the way down so it rests in the glue.

3 Once the Styrofoam ball is secure, apply hot glue to each piece of Dubble Bubble and attach a row around the center of the Styrofoam ball. Continue to cover the ball with gum, leaving the very top exposed in the shape of circle. Alternate gum flavors as desired. Glue the red gumballs in exposed circle at the top of the ball.

Jolly Cocktails

You will need:

- 1 martini or margarita glass
- White shredded paper
- 1 Styrofoam disk
- 1 (1 lb.) bag solid or multi-colored Jolly Ranchers
- 50 to 60 quilters T-pins or straight pins
- 2 to 3 gum drops or gummy citrus wedges
- 1 bamboo skewer
- 1 cocktail spear
- Cocktail umbrella, optional

To Begin...

1 Place three to four Jolly Ranchers in the bottom of the glass and cover with shredded paper. Pull some of the paper up and out over the sides of the glass. Cut the Styrofoam disk to fit snugly in the glass and place on top of the paper so that ½″ to 1″ of the disk is exposed above the edge of the glass. Press down gently to secure Styrofoam and paper in glass.

2 Insert a pin through one end of a candy wrapper. Push pin into Styrofoam to affix candy. Starting at the bottom, place the candies in a single row around the outside and top of the Styrofoam. Repeat until disk is completely covered.

3 Break the bamboo skewer in half and discard one half. Thread the gum drops or citrus wedges onto the remaining half of the skewer. Insert the cocktail spear into the top of the gumdrops or citrus wedges. Insert the bamboo skewer into the bouquet so it appears that candies are speared. Insert a cocktail umbrella at the top of the bouquet to further garnish.

Note, since the gumdrops are not wrapped they may be exposed to the Styrofoam and should not be eaten.

A Sweet Ride

You will need:

- 1 square Styrofoam piece
- 1 toy truck
- Red shredded paper
- Hot glue gun
- 8 to 10 small candy bars
- 1 to 2 large candy bars
- 10 to 12 Popsicle sticks
- 2 to 3 suckers
- 2 to 3 quilters T-pins or straight pins
- 2 to 3 pieces of wrapped gum

1 Trim the Styrofoam piece to fit snugly in the toy truck bed. Place the Styrofoam piece in the truck. Cover the Styrofoam with red shredded paper. Press down gently to secure the Styrofoam and paper in the truck.

2 Using the hot glue gun, squeeze glue on the back of each wrapped candy bar and adhere a Popsicle stick to the glue. Once glued, lay the sticks, candy bar-side down on a flat surface to dry for 1 to 2 minutes.

3 Insert Popsicle sticks with candy bars into the Styrofoam in the toy truck bed. Large candy bars should go in the back; small bars toward the front. Insert a pin into one end of each gum wrapper. Affix the pin and gum to the Styrofoam at the front of the arrangement.

Variation:

For a fun girl's display, arrange this bouquet in a pink convertible doll car.

Bunny Beans

You will need:

- 1 to 2 Styrofoam pieces
- 1 basket with handles
- White shredded paper
- 3 lbs. orange jellybeans
- 6 (10") clear plastic pastry bags
- 6 pieces green pipe cleaner
- 6 (5" to 6") pieces green rick rack
- 2 to 3 (10" to 12") pieces ribbon, various colors and patterns

To Begin...

1 Trim Styrofoam to fit inside basket. Place Styrofoam in basket and cover with shredded paper. Placing Styrofoam in the basket will help to prop candy carrots up so they are more easily seen.

2 Fill a pastry bag ⅔ full with orange jelly beans. Gather the excess plastic to close the bag. Wrap a piece of green pipe cleaner around the opening of the pastry bag. Tie a piece of green rick rack around the pipe cleaner. Repeat process with remaining supplies to make six carrots.

3 Arrange the candy carrots in the basket on top of the white shredded paper. Tie the ribbon around the handles of the basket and trim ends as needed.

Box of Chocolate Lollipops

You will need:

- 1 square Styrofoam piece
- 1 square box
- White shredded paper
- 1 (30″ to 36″) piece of ribbon, optional
- 9 to 12 plastic drinking straws, various colors
- 9 to 12 squares chocolate almond bark
- 3 to 4 heavy plastic storage bags
- Multi-colored candy sprinkles
- Plastic wrap
- 9 to 12 (5″ to 6″) pieces thin ribbon, various colors

To Begin...

1 Trim Styrofoam piece to fit snugly in the square box. Place Styrofoam in box and cover with white shredded paper. Press down gently to secure the Styrofoam and shredded paper in the box. If desired, tie or attach ribbon around the box for an extra decorative accent.

2 Cut off the bendable section or top third of the straw and discard, set larger straw halves aside. Lay parchment paper out over the work area. Place two to three squares of chocolate almond bark in one of the plastic bags. Place bag in a microwave-safe bowl and melt chocolate in the bag for 1 to 2 minutes, stopping halfway through to turn bag over. Do not melt all the chocolate in one bag. The bag will get too heavy and may tear.

3 Squeeze the melted chocolate into one corner of the bag. Snip off ¼″ of the bag's corner. With one hand holding a straw on waxed paper, use the other hand to squeeze a round glob of chocolate onto the straw. As you squeeze the bag, chocolate will spread out into a circle. Stop squeezing the bag when lollipop has reached 2½″ to 3″ in diameter or desired size. One square of melted bark should make one chocolate lollipop; if two to three squares of chocolate are melted in one bag, two to three lollipops should be made. Proceed immediately to step 4.

4 Allow chocolate lollipops to harden slightly for 10 to 15 seconds before decorating with candy sprinkles. After decorating, let lollipops dry and harden completely for 5 to 10 minutes. Repeat steps 2, 3 and 4 with remaining supplies.

5 Once dry, arrange chocolate lollipops in prepared box by inserting the straws into the Styrofoam. Gently press down on straws until they are secure. Do not handle chocolate when arranging lollipops. Use only straws to adjust and arrange the bouquet.

Food Safety Tip:

Ingesting Styrofoam can be dangerous to one's health. Using candy or food that is not prewrapped in a display with a Styrofoam base can expose edible items to unsafe dust and particles. Chocolate lollipops should be wrapped in small pieces of plastic wrap and secured with ribbon or rick rack at the bottom before being inserted into the Styrofoam base. Another option is wrapping the Styrofoam in tin foil or plastic wrap before inserting it into the box or container.

Take a Little Peep of My Heart

Peep of my

You will need:

- 1 Styrofoam piece
- Long, narrow box
- White shredded paper
- 1 (30″ to 36″) piece ribbon, optional
- 4 to 6 (8″) lollipop sticks
- 4 to 6 (4″) lollipop sticks
- 4 to 6 white marshmallow heart Peeps
- 4 to 6 red marshmallow heart Peeps

- 4 to 6 squares chocolate almond bark
- 4 to 6 squares white almond bark
- Red, white, pink and/or brown candy sprinkles
- Plastic wrap
- 8 (5″ to 6″) pieces red, white or pink rick rack

To Begin...

1 Trim Styrofoam piece to fit snugly in long narrow box. Place Styrofoam in box and cover with white shredded paper. Press down gently to secure the Styrofoam and shredded paper in the box. If desired, tie or attach ribbon around box for an extra decorative accent.

2 Remove marshmallows from package and gently tear apart. Scissors may be used to cut and trim hearts so shape is not lost. Insert one lollipop stick into the bottom of each marshmallow heart. Thread the stick only halfway through the heart so stick is not exposed at the top.

3 Place the white and chocolate almond bark in separate small bowls; melt in the microwave for 1 to 2 minutes, stopping once or twice to stir. Immerse hearts completely or halfway in either white or chocolate almond bark. A spoon may be used to smooth and cover the hearts. Proceed immediately to step 4.

4 Place chocolate dipped hearts flat on a piece of waxed paper; allow chocolate to harden for 10 to 15 seconds before decorating with candy sprinkles. After decorating, let hearts dry and harden completely for 5 to 10 minutes.

5 Once dry, arrange dipped hearts in box by inserting the lollipop sticks into the Styrofoam. Gently press sticks into the Styrofoam to secure. Place tall hearts toward the back and short hearts toward the front.

Food Safety Tip:

Ingesting Styrofoam can be dangerous to one's health. Using candy or food that is not pre-wrapped in a display with a Styrofoam base can expose edible items to unsafe dust and particles. Chocolate dipped hearts should be wrapped in small pieces of plastic wrap and secured with ribbon or rick rack at the bottom before being inserted into the Styrofoam base. Another option is wrapping the Styrofoam in foil or plastic wrap before inserting it into the box or container.

Just What the Doctor Ordered

You will need:

- Hot glue gun
- 1 (3″ x 2″) Styrofoam disk
- 1 (8 oz.) can Dr. Pepper
- 1 (1 lb.) bag Soda Poppers hard candies
- 50 to 60 quilters T-pins or straight pins

To Begin...

1 Using the glue gun, squeeze glue on one flat side of the Styrofoam disk. Attach the disk to the top of the Dr. Pepper can; let dry for 3 to 5 to minutes.

2 Insert a pin through one end of the candy wrapper and affix pin and candy to the Styrofoam. Starting at the bottom, place the candies in single rows around the outside and top of the Styrofoam. Repeat until top and sides of disk are completely covered. Alternate candy flavors as desired.

Variation:

Try using different types of soft drinks and different sized cans. Tootsie Rolls, miniature Snickers and miniature MilkyWays are all tasty options to decorate the can. For health-conscious friends, canned diet drinks and sugar-free hard candies are great for sweet but lighter arrangements.

You will need:

- 1 beer mug
- 1½ (1 lb.) bags root beer candies
- 1 Styrofoam disk
- White shredded paper
- 50 to 70 quilters T-pins or straight pins
- 4 to 5 Dum Dum suckers, cola or root beer flavored
- 1 plastic bendable straw

To Begin...

1 Fill the beer mug ⅔ full with root beer candies. Cover the candies with white shredded paper. Pull some of the shredded paper up and out over the sides of the mug. Trim the Styrofoam disk to fit snugly in the mug. Insert disk into mug so that ½" to 1" of the disk is exposed above the edge of the mug. Press down gently to secure disk in the mug.

2 Insert a pin through one end of each candy wrapper. Push pin into Styrofoam to affix candy. Place the candies in single rows around the outside and top of the disk. Repeat until sides of disk are completely covered and there is a small circle exposed at the top.

3 Insert the cola or root beer flavored suckers into exposed Styrofoam. Press down gently so only the wrappers are exposed above the other candy. Cut the bottom third off the straw and discard. Insert the remaining top ⅔ of the straw between candies and into the Styrofoam disk, pressing down gently to secure. Bend straw at an angle.

Super Sweet &
Sugar Free

You will need:

- 1 Styrofoam disk
- 1 coffee mug
- Excelsior moss
- Hot glue gun
- 12 to 14 Popsicle sticks
- 12 to 14 pieces sugar-free candy

To Begin...

1 Trim Styrofoam disk to fit snugly in coffee mug. Insert Styrofoam disk into the mug and cover with moss. Press down gently to secure the Styrofoam and moss in the coffee mug.

2 Using the hot glue gun, squeeze glue on the back of each candy piece and adhere a Popsicle stick to the glue. Once glued, lay the sticks, candy-side down on a flat surface to dry for 1 to 2 minutes.

3 Insert Popsicle sticks in the Styrofoam in the coffee mug. At the front of arrangement, press candy all the way into Styrofoam. Press second row of candy ⅔ of the way into Styrofoam. Place third row halfway into Styrofoam. And, press final and fourth row only ⅓ of the way into Styrofoam. This will create a layered effect in the arrangement. Fan candies out slightly while arranging. If the arrangement will be displayed as a centerpiece, and Popsicle sticks should not be seen in the back, place candy in a circle around the edge of the mug and layer as directed above.

Baby Cakes

You will need:

- 1 (3″ x 2″) Styrofoam disk
- Hot glue gun
- 9 to 10 pieces grape Laffy Taffy
- White shredded paper
- 9 to 10 pink bubblegum Dum Dum suckers
- 4 to 5 blue raspberry Dum Dum suckers
- 1 cherry or strawberry Dum Dum sucker
- 1 (10″ to 12″) piece pink ribbon or rick rack

1 Using the hot glue gun, squeeze hot glue on the back of one Laffy Taffy; attach to the Styrofoam disk. Line the end of the taffy up with the bottom of the disk so it sits level. The taffy wrappers will extend higher than Styrofoam. Repeat with remaining taffy until outside of disk is covered.

2 Cover the top of the disk with white shredded paper, pulling the ends slightly over the top of the taffy wrappers. Insert the pink bubblegum suckers in a circle around the outer part of the Styrofoam disk. Insert the blue raspberry suckers into Styrofoam inside of the pink and standing up a little higher.

3 Unwrap the cherry or strawberry sucker and insert it into the middle of the Styrofoam disk a little higher than the blue suckers. Wrap or tie the pink rick rack or ribbon around the outside of the candy cupcake.

Note, since red sucker is not wrapped, it may be exposed to the Styrofoam particles and should not be eaten.

Sweet
Peppermint Tree

You will need:

- 2 (1 lb.) bags peppermint swirl candies
- 1 (10″ tall) Styrofoam cone
- 15 to 20 red cinnamon candies
- 100 to 150 quilters T-pins
- 2 to 3 (10″ to 12″) pieces ribbon and/or rick rack, various colors and patterns
- 3 small jingle bells

To Begin...

1 Insert a T-pin through one end of a candy wrapper. Push pin into Styrofoam to affix candy to cone. Place candies in a single row, circling the cone completely. Repeat until the cone is completely covered. Leave a small space at the very top of the cone exposed in order to decorate top with ribbon. Randomly pin red cinnamon candies around the cone for an extra decorative accent.

2 Fold some of the ribbon pieces in half to create loops and leave others straight. Arrange the ribbon to look like a bow or other creative display. Place a pin in the center of the ribbon arrangement and affix to the top of the cone. Once attached, trim ribbon to fit cone as desired.

3 Insert T-pins through the bottom of the jingle bells and pull the sharp end through the opening on the other side. Affix the bells to the top of the cone, covering the center of the ribbon arrangement.

Let's Go
to the Movies

You will need:

- 1 Styrofoam piece
- 1 plastic or cardboard popcorn container
- Red shredded paper
- Hot glue gun

- 8 to 10 small candy bars
- 5 to 7 large candy bars
- 13 to 15 Popsicle sticks
- 1 to 2 suckers

To Begin...

1 Trim the Styrofoam to fit snugly in the popcorn container. Insert the Styrofoam into the container and press down gently so there is ½″ between the top of the container and the Styrofoam. Cover Styrofoam with red shredded paper. Pull some of the shredded paper up and out over the sides of the container.

2 Using the hot glue gun, squeeze glue on the back of each candy bar and adhere a Popsicle stick to the glue. Once glued, lay the sticks, candy bar-side down, on a flat surface to dry for 1 to 2 minutes.

3 Insert Popsicle sticks into the Styrofoam in the popcorn container, placing large candy bars in the back and small candy bars toward the front. Arrange candy bars so they fan out slightly. Insert suckers into the arrangement to fill in empty spaces and holes. If the arrangement will be displayed as centerpiece and Popsicle sticks should not be seen in the back, place candy in a circle around the edge of the container with large candy bars in the middle and small on the outside.

You will need:

- 1 to 2 (10″ to 12″) pieces ribbon, various colors and patterns
- 1 sundae or parfait glass
- 1 (1 lb.) bag miniature MilkyWays
- Cream-colored shredded paper
- 1 Styrofoam disk
- 50 to 60 quilters T-pins or straight pins
- 1 cherry or strawberry Tootsie Pop sucker

To Begin...

1 Tie ribbon around the stem of the sundae or parfait glass. Place two to three miniature MilkyWays in the bottom of the glass. Cover the MilkyWays with cream-colored shredded paper. Pull some of the shredded paper up and over the sides of the glass. Trim the Styrofoam disk to fit snugly in the glass. Insert disk into the glass so that ½″ to 1″ of the disk is exposed above the edge of the glass. Press down gently to secure the Styrofoam disk in the glass.

2 Insert a pin through one end of a MilkyWay wrapper. Push pin into Styrofoam to affix candy. Place the MilkyWays in a single row around the outside and top of the Styrofoam. Repeat until sides of disk are completely covered and there is only a small portion exposed at the top.

3 Insert the Tootsie Pop sucker into the center of the exposed area on the Styrofoam disk. Press down gently until only the red wrapper of the sucker shows above the MilkyWays.

You will need:

- 1 Styrofoam ball
- 1 coconut glass, straw and silk flowers optional
- White shredded paper, optional
- 1 (1 lb.) bag Life Savers, Piña Colada, Coconut and Banana flavors only
- 30 to 40 quilters T-pins or straight pins
- 1 drink umbrella, optional

To Begin...

1 Trim off a small end of the Styrofoam ball, discard remaining piece. Place the Styrofoam, rounded side down, into the coconut glass so the top of the Styrofoam is flush with the top of the glass. If desired, cover Styrofoam with white shredded paper. Pull the paper down over the sides of the coconut cup. Decorate cup with silk flowers, as desired.

2 Insert a pin through one end of the Life Saver wrapper. Push pin into Styrofoam to affix candy. Place the candies in a single row around the Styrofoam. Repeat until the Styrofoam is completely covered. Alternate Life Saver flavors as desired.

3 Insert the cocktail umbrella into the Styrofoam and press down gently to secure. Decorate arrangement with a straw as desired. See page 29 for directions.

You will need:

- 1 Styrofoam disk
- 1 small galvanized pail
- Red shredded paper
- 4 to 6 small candy bars with red, white and/or blue wrappers
- 1 to 2 large candy bars with red, white and/or blue wrappers
- 1 (20″ to 24″) piece red, white and blue ribbon

To Begin...

1. Trim the Styrofoam disk so it will slide all the way down into the pail and fit snugly at the bottom. Cover Styrofoam with red shredded paper. Pull some of the shredded paper up and over the sides of the pail. Set some paper aside for later.

2. Using the hot glue gun, squeeze glue on the back of each candy bar and adhere a Popsicle stick to the glue. Once glued, lay the sticks, candy bar-side down on a flat surface to dry for 1 to 2 minutes.

3. Insert the Popsicle sticks into the Styrofoam in the pail, placing large candy bars in the back and small candy bars toward the front. Arrange candy bars so they fan out slightly. Insert remaining shredded paper into any exposed holes. If the arrangement will be displayed as a centerpiece and Popsicle sticks should not be seen in the back, place candy in a circle around the edge of the pail with large candy bars in the middle and small ones on the outside.

Lollipop Malt

Lollipop
Malt

You will need:

- 1 (12″ to 16″) piece ribbon, any pattern or color
- 1 milkshake glass
- 1 small Styrofoam ball
- White shredded paper
- 32 Dum Dum suckers, assorted flavors
- 12 Blow Pop suckers
- 7 pink Tootsie Pop suckers
- 1 strawberry or raspberry Tootsie Pop sucker
- 1 bendable plastic straw
- 4 to 5 (5″ to 6″) pieces rick rack, assorted colors

To Begin...

1 Tie the ribbon around the stem of the milkshake glass. Insert the Styrofoam ball all the way into the milkshake glass and cover with white shredded paper. Pull some of the paper up and out over the sides of the glass.

2 Insert Dum Dum suckers into the Styrofoam ball, arranging suckers in two rows around the outside edge of the milkshake glass. Second row should be slightly higher than the one before it. In the same manner, insert a single row of Blow Pops slightly higher than the Dum Dum Suckers. Then insert a single row of pink Tootsie Pop suckers slightly higher than the Blow Pops. Finally insert the strawberry or raspberry Tootsie Pop in the very top of the Styrofoam ball. Once completed, only sucker wrappers should be exposed.

3 Cut the bottom ⅓ off the straw and discard. Insert the remaining ⅔ of the straw between suckers and into the Styrofoam ball; press down gently to secure. Insert pieces of rick rack in between suckers around the outside edges of the glass.

Hearty Bouquet

You will need:

- 7 (10″) bamboo skewers
- Green florist tape
- 4 red marshmallow heart Peeps
- 4 (5″ to 6″) pieces ribbon, various colors and patterns
- 6 to 9 white gumdrops
- 1 small vase
- 4 to 6 (5″ to 6″) pieces green rick rack

To Begin...

1 Cut ends off six of the bamboo skewers so each one is a different height. Wrap each skewer in florist tape leaving only the tapered end slightly exposed.

2 Insert tapered end of a skewer into each of the heart Peeps. Tie a piece of ribbon around each of the skewers at the base of the heart. Thread two to three gumdrops on the remaining skewers.

3 Insert skewers into the vase and arrange so tall skewers are in the back and short skewers are in the front. Insert pieces of green rick rack around the outer edge of the vase.

Dum Dum Daisies
Daisies

You will need:

- 1 small Styrofoam disk
- 1 (2½″ tall) terra cotta pot
- 1 piece green tissue paper
- White shredded paper
- 3 to 4 pieces heavy solid paper, various colors
- 3 to 4 pieces heavy patterned paper, various colors and patterns
- 1 piece heavy green paper
- Paper punch
- 3 to 4 Dum Dum suckers, any flavor
- 3 to 4 pieces white pipe cleaner

To Begin...

1 Trim the Styrofoam disk to fit snugly in the terra cotta pot. Insert the disk into the pot and cover with white shredded paper. Pull some of the shredded paper up and out over the sides of the pot. Press down gently to secure the disk and shredded paper in the pot.

2 Cut out one small circle of the green tissue paper. Cut small tabs all around the circles to make a fringed edge; set aside. Fold both a piece of solid and patterned paper in half and cut five shapes of half a heart on the fold of each. Cut one leaf shape out of the green paper. Punch a hole in the bottom of each heart closest to the point and at one end of the leaf shape. Punch a hole in the center of the tissue paper circle. Thread onto the Dum Dum stick beginning with tissue paper circle, then five patterned hearts, then five solid hearts and ending with one leaf. Secure paper by wrapping a pipe cleaner around the Dum Dum stick as close to the sucker as possible. Repeat with remaining supplies.

3 Fan out the hearts to look like petals of a flower. Insert the flowers into the prepared pot and arrange as desired.

Note: With the help of an adult, this is a great bouquet or craft for children to make.

You will need:

- 1 Styrofoam ball
- 1 (5½" tall) container
- Excelsior moss
- 1 (20" to 24") piece ribbon, any color or pattern
- 8 to 10 (12") bamboo skewers
- 3 (7.5 oz.) bags butterscotch disks
- Florist tape
- 16 to 18 (10") bamboo skewers

To Begin...

1 Trim the Styrofoam ball to fit snugly in the container. Insert ball into container and cover with excelsior moss. Press down gently to secure the ball and moss in the container. Tie ribbon around the container.

2 Beginning with the 12″ skewers, hold one butterscotch disk at the top of the skewer and begin to wrap the florist tape around both the candy wrapper and skewer until candy is securely attached. Continue wrapping tape down the skewer. Halfway down, hold another piece of candy next to the skewer and wrap florist tape around both the candy wrapper and skewer. Repeat with another candy disk about 1½″ below the second. Once three pieces of candy are attached, wrap the skewer completely in florist tape leaving only the tapered end of the skewer exposed. Repeat with remaining skewers and candy. When wrapping 10″ skewers, attach only one or two butterscotch disks.

3 Insert the skewers into the Styrofoam in the prepared container. Arrange bouquet so tall skewers are in the center and short skewers are around the outside edge. Arrange skewers so they fan out slightly.

You will need:

- ½ C. green M&Ms, peanut or milk chocolate
- 1½ C. blue M&Ms, peanut or milk chocolate
- 1 small fish bowl or bud vase
- 1 (12.6 oz.) bag Swedish Fish AquaLife Candy
- 3 (8″) lollipop sticks
- 3 (5″ to 6″) pieces blue ribbon

To Begin...

1 Place the green M&Ms in the bottom of the bowl or bud vase. Place the blue M&Ms on top of the green M&Ms.

2 Gently slide Swedish Fish candies down the inner edges of the glass. Wedge the candies between the bowl and the M&Ms so candies stay suspended and do not sink to the bottom of the bowl or vase. Alternate candy shapes as desired.

3 Slide one fish candy onto each of the three lollipop sticks. If desired, cut the lollipop sticks to different heights. Tie a blue ribbon around each stick at the base of the fish. Insert sticks into the M&Ms in the bowl or vase. Arrange sticks so they fan out slightly.

Variation:

Don't stop at a small bowl; try this arrangement with a full-size fish bowl. It makes a great centerpiece. Instead of using M&Ms, try using jelly beans, Skittles or any other brightly-colored candy.

Golden Globe
Topiary

You will need:

- Gold metallic spray paint
- 1 (8″) Styrofoam ball
- 1 (6″) Styrofoam ball
- 1 (6½″) flower pot, any color
- 1 (24″) piece contorted willow

- Hot glue gun
- Excelsior moss
- 1 (40 oz.) bag miniature peanut butter cups
- 1 to 2 (26″ to 30″) pieces ribbon, various colors and patterns

To Begin...

1 Spray half of the 8″ Styrofoam ball with gold metallic spray paint. Allow to dry at least 30 minutes to 1 hour. Once dry, spray other half of the ball with gold paint. Ball will need at least two to three total coats of paint. Allow 1 to 2 hours for both sides to dry completely.

2 Insert the 6″ Styrofoam ball snuggly into the flower pot. Press down gently to secure ball in pot. Apply hot glue to the end of the willow piece and insert into the center of the Styrofoam ball in the pot. The glue will dry and keep the willow stable and in place. Apply glue to the top of the willow piece. Slide the painted Styrofoam ball ⅓ of the way down on the willow piece. Cover the ball in the flower pot with excelsior moss.

3 Apply a dot of hot glue to one miniature peanut butter cup at a time. Then attach the peanut butter cup to the painted ball. Cover the Styrofoam ball completely with peanut butter cups, placing them as close to each other as possible. Tie the ribbon around the contorted willow.

Note: When creating a topiary with more than one ball, it's better to attach candy to Styrofoam first and then slide balls onto dowels. See topiary on pages 5 through 7 for directions.

Sweet Baby

You will need:

- 1 (4 to 5 oz.) baby bottle
- ½ C. Smoothie Mix Skittles
- White shredded paper
- Hot glue gun
- 1 (2½″) Styrofoam ball
- 5 (2.75 oz.) bags Life Savers sugar-free Sorbets
- 40 to 60 quilters T-pins or straight pins
- 1 to 2 (12″ to 16″) pieces ribbon, various colors and patterns

1 Remove the top and nipple from the bottle. Fill bottle with Skittles. Place a small amount of white shredded paper over the skittles in the neck of the bottle. Squeeze hot glue onto the Styrofoam ball and attach it to the open end of the bottle. Allow to dry completely for 5 to 10 minutes.

2 Insert a pin through one end of each Life Saver wrapper and affix pin and candy to the ball. Starting at the bottom, place the Life Savers in single rows around the ball. Repeat until the ball is covered, leaving a circle the same size as the bottle lid exposed at the top. Alternate Life Saver flavors as desired.

3 Tie ribbon around the bottle lid just below the nipple. Insert a small amount of white shredded paper into the nipple. Squeeze hot glue around the bottom edge of the bottle lid and attach it to the top of the Styrofoam ball. Hold in place for 1 to 2 minutes until secure; allow to dry completely for 5 to 10 minutes. Do not lift arrangement by the bottle lid as glue might not hold the weight of the candy-filled bottle.

You will need:

- 1 Styrofoam disk
- 1 coffee cup
- White shredded paper, optional
- 2 squares chocolate almond bark
- 2 to 3 plastic spoons
- Multi-colored candy sprinkles
- 50 to 60 quilters T-pins or straight pins

- 2 (4 oz.) boxes Nips coffee candy
- 2 (4 oz.) boxes Nips caramel candy
- 3 Bogdon old fashioned candy sticks
- Plastic wrap
- 2 to 3 (5″ to 6″) pieces brown ribbon

To Begin...

1 Trim Styrofoam disk to fit snugly in coffee cup. Insert disk into coffee cup so that ½ to 1" of the disk is exposed above the edge of the cup. Press down gently to secure disk in cup. If desired, cover the Styrofoam with white shredded paper. Pull some of the shredded paper down over the sides of the cup.

2 Place the chocolate almond bark in a small microwave-safe bowl and melt in the microwave for 1 to 2 minutes, stopping halfway through to stir. Dip the "bowl" of one plastic spoon into the chocolate, covering both sides. Hold spoon upright to harden for 5 to 10 seconds; decorate with candy sprinkles and gently lay on waxed paper to dry for 5 to 10 minutes. Repeat with remaining spoons, almond bark and sprinkles.

3 Insert a pin through one end of each Nips wrapper. Push pin into Styrofoam to affix candy. Place the candies in single rows around the outside and top of the Styrofoam. Repeat, alternating coffee and caramel flavors, until sides of disk are completely covered and there is only a small oval-shaped portion exposed at the top.

4 Insert a pin through the end of one candy stick wrapper. Push pin into the top of Styrofoam to affix candy stick. Because of the stiffness of the wrapper, the candy stick will stand upright. Repeat with remaining two candy sticks, fanning sticks out while arranging. Insert chocolate covered spoons' handles into Styrofoam behind the candy sticks in the remaining space on top of the disk. Press down on spoons gently to secure.

Food Safety Tip:

Ingesting Styrofoam can be dangerous to one's health. Using candy or food that is not pre-wrapped in a display with a Styrofoam base can expose edible items to unsafe dust and particles. Chocolate-dipped spoons should be wrapped in small pieces of plastic wrap and secured with ribbon at the bottom before being inserted into the Styrofoam base. Another option is wrapping the Styrofoam in foil or plastic wrap before inserting it in the coffee cup.